The Moon

by Martha E. H. Rustad

raintree

a Capstone company — publishers for children

Raintree is an imprint of Capstone Global Library Limited, a company incorporated in England and Wales having its registered office at 264 Banbury Road, Oxford, OX2 7DY – Registered company number: 6695582

www.raintree.co.uk
myorders@raintree.co.uk

Edited by Erika L. Shores
Designed by Juliette Peters and Katelin Plekkenpol
Picture research by Tracy Cummins
Production by Katy LaVigne
Originated by Capstone Global Library
Printed and bound in China.

ISBN 978 1 4747 1251 4

19 18 17 16 15
10 9 8 7 6 5 4 3 2 1

British Library Cataloguing in Publication Data
A full catalogue record for this book is available from the British Library.

Acknowledgements
We would like to thank the following for permission to reproduce photographs:
Science Source: Gary Hincks, 7; Shutterstock: Aphelleon, 15, godrick, cover, 1, Kalenik Hanna, Design Element, Keith Publicover, 9, Sarun T, 21, Suppakij1017, 5, Tom Reichner, 18-19, 19 right, Tristan3D, 11, Wikimedia: Jay Tanner, 17, NASA, 13.

Every effort has been made to contact copyright holders of material reproduced in this book. Any omissions will be rectified in subsequent printings if notice is given to the publisher.

All the internet addresses (URLs) given in this book were valid at the time of going to press. However, due to the dynamic nature of the internet, some addresses may have changed, or sites may have changed or ceased to exist since publication. While the author and publisher regret any inconvenience this may cause readers, no responsibility for any such changes can be accepted by either the author or the publisher.

Editor's Note
In this book's photographs, the sizes of objects and the distances between them are not to scale.

Contents

In the sky

A full Moon shines.

It glows at night.

What is the Moon?

It is a big round rock!

A moon orbits a planet.

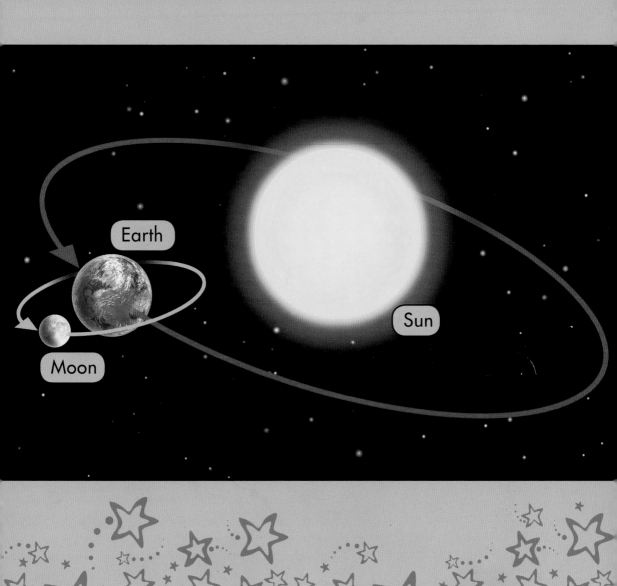

Earth

Sun

Moon

The Moon is 384,600 kilometres (239,000 miles) away from Earth. What if we could drive there? It would take 153 days!

A big rock

The Moon is 3,476 km
(2,160 miles) wide.
Four Moons could fit
inside Earth.

MOON

EARTH

Dust covers the Moon.

It has craters all over it.

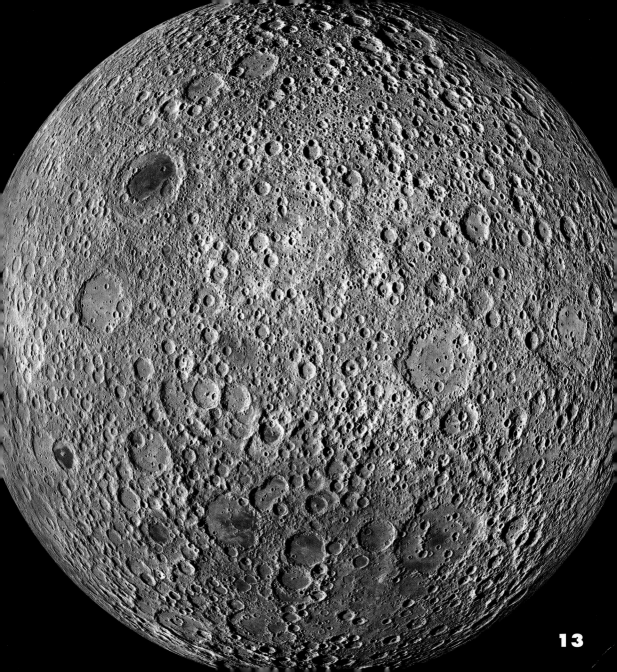

The Moon and Earth

Sunlight hits the Moon.
The light bounces back
to Earth.

Half of the Moon is
very hot.
Half is very cold.

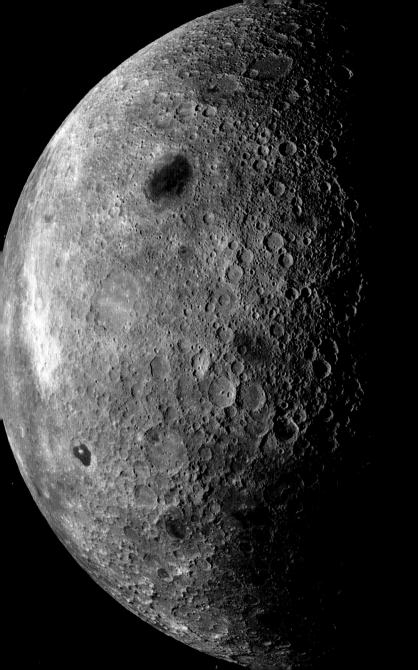

How much of the Moon

do we see?

It is always changing.

Look! A full Moon.

Look! A crescent Moon.

Earth needs the Moon.

It pulls ocean tides.

Thank you, Moon!

Glossary

crater large, bowl-shaped hole

orbit follow a curved path around an object in space

planet large object in space that orbits a star

tide rising and falling of ocean water; tides move twice each day

Find out more

On the Moon (First Reading Level 1), Anna Milbourne (Usborne, 2011)

The Moon (Space), Ian Graham (Raintree, 2010)

Websites

solarsystem.nasa.gov/planets/profile.cfm?Object=Moon
Find out facts about Earth's Moon on this website.

www.bbc.co.uk/education/clips/zj3ygk7
Visit this website to watch a video about the Moon.

Index